HANAN SAYS:

The rediscovered poetry and aphorisms of

Hanan al Hannan

Revealed and Written by Jef Buehler

1/09

Lisa Eve ☺

May you and your path continue to rediscover each other with joy and fulfilling mystery.

Love, Jef

In the center of your heart

The seed of the All

The seed of the One

Grows into that which it already is

And will be

LA I'LLAHA I'LLAH ALLAHU

There is No God But God

DEDICATION

While there are many, many people in this lifetime who deserve thanks for being part of my (and Hanan's) journey to these pages, this edition of **Hanan Says:** *is simply and humbly dedicated to* **David La Chapelle,** *citizen of this world and the Universe, facilitator of growth, translator of feeling, teacher of being real and present to beings far and wide. David's gift is and has been to help others see what they need to see, hear what they need to hear, heal what they need to heal and, ultimately, be who they are. As a teacher he is fiercely patient and – as sometimes needed -- lovingly stern. Beyond writing numerous articles, he is the author of* **Navigating the Tides of Change** *and the* **Destiny Lines** *audio book, a wonderful and goofy singer, guitar player and chanter, and just about the kindest guy you could ever hope to know.*

At the time of this writing, he is also now in need of much care, love, support and prayer as continues an intense physical and energetic dialogue with a serious illness.

Hanan Says: *has been in a state of perpetual incubation for almost three years now and has never seemed complete. However, once I learned of David's struggles, Hanan very clearly kicked me in the metaphoric butt to complete this book and share it immediately, in its current form, regardless of my opinion of it being done or good enough.*

Thank you, David. May the energy, love and hope that comes from any or all of this hold you and keep you.

A portion of all sales of this book will be donated to support David La Chapelle's wellness and wellbeing.

Thanksgiving, November 2008

AUTHOR'S NOTE

People ask me if Hanan al Hannan is a fictitious person, and if the works herein are fiction. Not wishing to either obfuscate or disappoint, I must reply: On a literal level, the answer is yes. But this question begs another: What *is* fiction, anyway?

Is fiction something untrue, or a deception?

If so, much of history as we know it must be considered fiction, even as we are taught to believe it and consider it almost sacrosanct fact. Ask the Taino natives of the Caribbean about their account of history around 1492 and it surely appears radically different than most of our readings of Columbus' era then and now. Try to define what is historical reality and fiction among the numerous perspectives of Jews and Palestinians, Americans and Iraqis, and even *within* America regarding current and millennia-old issues and conflicts in the Middle East.

We as a nation have just begun the process of reinterpreting our long-term and daily "history" in democratically electing a President in whose persona and within whose vision is held some of the antidote for at least the past eight years of fear, deception and division. This change is happening in spite of finite definitions of America and being an American that have been both bred into us over generations and then strategically (I would offer, maliciously) targeted and subconsciously followed by the majority of our population. The conglomeration of subtle, pervasive and filtered ways of looking at reality that author/philosopher Daniel Quinn so aptly describes in *Ishmael* and his other works as Mother Culture is very much at work here, yet is broken down to what I would call multiple "Aunt- and

1

Uncle Cultures" that, as this recent election and transition has shown, further complicate matters of what is real – or not. Where you *stand* so often is tied to where you *sit*.

When Hanan decided to speak through me, to enter my being and inform me about his life and what he said during that life I had three choices: I could attempt to fight it actively (e.g., take sleeping pills, get drunk); I could attack it passively (e.g., distract and numb myself with work, TV and other media, etc.); or I could ride it out, be with it and see what might happen. Five sleepless days and nights later I found I had midwived twenty-some poems, much of Hanan's life-story, his historical context and a sense that the Universe was not done yet. The contrast between what I thought was my path and *raison d'etre* and the joyful, unnerving, exhausting and ecstatic experience of Hanan using me as a vessel for his work was stark beyond description. The only antidote was and is to keep hearing Hanan, translating his words from 14th Century Farsi and writing them down. The All had spoken: *this* is my job.

Or at least, *was*. Almost three years later, the situation has evolved and shifted in unexpected ways: having not actually slept for about two of those years, having gone through about every life-change imaginable outside of serious injury or death during that time, having remarried and become a father, it turns out that being the vessel for Hanan is more of a *part-time* job.   So it is that the sharing of his poetry in the form of this book may only be a portion of the story. Nonetheless, it is the part whose time it is ripe to share.

This book is divided into the four elemental quadrants – Air, Fire, Water and Earth – that in Hanan's time and Sufi culture served as one of the archetypes used to define the four chambers of the animal and

2

human heart. Over time, Hanan's poems have found their instinctual homes in their respective elements. Oftentimes this orchestration occurred against my intellectual efforts and interpretations. After several attempts to rearrange the spiritual furniture, I finally just let go of my will and allowed the flow, to, well, flow.

I do not claim to know the ultimate truth of even my own history, let alone that of the global theater known as Earth. Yet, what if the expressions of experience and interpretations of life that coursed through me in the birthing of *Hanan Says:* are as true to me as their chosen vessel and recorder as an apple I hold in my hand? For me, their form and taste are real and equally there.

Is *Hanan Says:* fiction? To me, no: it is both real and does not matter. If your reading of this book results in inspiration, reflection or otherwise helps you see the nearness of your path and the paths of others then *that* real truth supercedes any literary categorization of this work.

I believe, more than anything, that what Hanan says is valid both for his time, our present and the future. Equally, I believe that we all have inner voices and sounds, connected in some way to something greater, some source beyond our complete grasping. When we listen to what comes, swimming so often against seemingly strong and surrounding currents of everyday life, we move closer to the specific path to our purpose, to treating ourselves and others as imperfect and lovable seekers on that journey, and maybe, just maybe, get to follow the breadcrumbs to peek behind the curtain and see that which is not yet revealed.

With peace, love and gratitude, Jef Buehler

POEMS
&
APHORISMS

Hanan says:

Be careful what
You wish for...
God is already twirling around and
Through us as she
Dances her formless
All in and out
Of our sight, smell,
Taste and touch
Laughing a trail of planets and galaxies,
Rainbows and amoeba
In her wake.
Wishing only gives her
Incentive
To come up with
A more confounding riddle
To the answer we already know.

Hanan Says:

Hallelujah!
We are all shards of God
Pieces of the beautiful and ethereal All.
But then we go through this lifetime
Surprised to find that each of us is rough around the edges.

Hanan says:

Is God
Allah, Jesus
Or Buddha?
No.
God is a dung beetle,
Blade of grass or pebble.

Do not worry
Dear seeker
About naming God

Spend your gifts
That God may
Be known in your name.

Hanan Says:

Stars puncture the amber-rust and darkening sky
The sun still shines
Mist settles in over orchards in the valley
The sun still shines
You take your prayers in the tent's shade at mid-day
The sun still shines
Eyelids close of man and beast, blotting out the light
The sun still shines

The sun always shines, Pilgrim
Even as we may not see it

Hanan says:

Don't you tell me
What I don't know —
I know what that is
Even if the knowing
Of the unknown is
Both beyond and within
The knowledge known to
Us all and God.
Let me wallow in my
Pretend cloak of
Ignorance until I am
Ready to burst from
My shell and shout the
Truth of my naked
Bloom under the sun and
Stars of my heart.

Beloved:

I make you sit with me long hours
Under the turning of the night sky
That you may feel at home
With the expansiveness
Of your own heart

Hanan says:

Man is an ingenious animal
He thinks he can dictate
How things are to *be*
Instead of being
With how things (actually) are
Letting God's inhale
And exhale
Of each moment
Be prayer enough

Hanan says:

Of course God is
A "She".
Would a male
Be likely able to juggle
The myriad millions of beings
Billions of forms
And zillions of pieces
Of the One
Staying remotely conscious and
Keeping a sense of humor
Over infinite time?

Actually, yes.
But He took a
Easier job at the smaller
Universe next door.

Hanan says:

Have you ever made love
To light?
Inhaled the sunrise with
A kiss?
Slow-danced with a chorus line
Of candle flames?
Read poetry over
Wine to the stars and
Moon
After your celestial orgy
Had subsided?

Light wears many forms of negligee:
Glimmers, reflections
Flickers, refractions
And it is safe to say Light
Goes both ways.
But remember that Light
Is God's breath, lest you
Think you can get
Away with a
Quickie.

Hanan Says:

Thy scent and spirit
Open the sky
Releasing the stars of desire
While fire in your eye
Hangs above
A landscape soon to be all the poorer
For your absence

Hanan says:

I woke up
South of midnight
Mind modulating
Digesting and burping
A day's worth of soul learning
That, unbeknownst to me
Would, some twenty hours later,
Birth this poem
For all to hear.

As we leave a temporal trail of feet and hooves
Open space lies before us
Open sky in shaded hues of blues and blacks above
Filled with nothing
Filled with nothing but air
In whose infinitely imperceptible womb
Is held such that is unseen yet essential for life

As we breathe we live

God has given the gift of breath and
Made it so easy
That we must work to *not* breathe!
All men share that same air
Stand they shoulder to shoulder
Or in distant towns and empires
And are connected to each other

As they live they breathe

Bound together by invisible strands
Inhaling and exhaling the All's kindness and love
Taking in the All itself as we respire

It is a long journey tonight -
Recline on my coarse blanket
Allow your eyelids to lapse at their guard
Let God infuse your waking dream
Reuniting you, one breath at a time,
With your Home

Hanan says:

Angels dervish dance
When we
Are not looking
Like mice having
Gotten into the flour
Leaving myriad tracks
Before the Owner awakens

Hanan says:

In the Word
Is the seed of form —
In this moment of time
This perceived place —
Like a speck of dust on
Fibers in the
Lint of the
Bellybutton of the Universe
Our forms
Are carried
By the
Greatness
Of the
One

I don't mean to imply that I
Know
You, Beloved

I only mean to say
That jumping into the void together
Laughing, crying – Being (alive)
Has made me a firm believer in gravity!

As long as we get to
Hold our hands and hearts along the way,
I bet this will work out just fine.

In fact, that is the whole point
Of this Love-exercise.

Sunshine:

A glance in the flickering and shifting air
Mirrored in the molecules of space
Between your smile
And my eyes
Traverses that distance
In a blink of the present moment
Like some ship filled with intent
To complete its mission
Over months of blackness and unknown
Perforated by stars alone
Setting alight
Through its purposeful flight
The source
Without which life
Fades from our sight...

Love sometimes blooms
In strange places
Bringing flowers of passion
Intense interest and intent
Out of seemingly nowhere
Or so we allow ourselves to think.
In truth
We are all part of the One
Spinning about in perceived
Separate lives
In
Or out of Love's orbit
Feeling stunned by the strength
Of its gravity.
God laughs at our discernments and analysis
She knows we are but fingers and toes
Of the same body
Born and fed from the source that is the All.

Hanan Says:

Locusts' rhythm
Circadian and certain
Permeates every sweaty pore
As the day wanes to evening
A long, smooth exhale of heat
Sighing into the waiting arms
Of the dark Queen
Languidly awaiting us for a brief kiss
Swathed in her bejeweled robes

Your scent
Last overt vestige of
Our yesterday
Lingers
Hastily embroidered
On the pillow
Next to me
Your love
The energy and life
You shared
While here
Will not fade
However
Only grows
And welcomes me back
Every time I return, Beloved
Opening the door to my heart
For which you so joyously
And freely have been the key

Hanan Says:

Directing your attention to something or someone
Makes all the difference.
Being present,
Focusing ones thoughts, feelings and energy
Intensely
Heightening your connection to each other
Grants you the merest fraction of an idea
Of what it is like to be God
And that's on a good day!

Hanan Says:

Your gait
Your breath
Your heartbeat
Entwined in the tapestry of your laughter
Form the cadence of the poem
That is you,
Beloved.

Let me read you.
Let me read you again.

Hanan says:

Did you ever notice how
Candles
Burn up
And down
At the same time
Like wax-filled
Yogis
With karma to spare?

Hanan says:

Notice the pistachio –
Until it is tested
By the flame
It will release
The sweet nut
Only by great force
And broken fingernails

Hanan says:

Be wary of holding tight the
Hot coal of anger in your breast
It may bring comfort, seeker
On a cold night
In the open plain
Giving you warmth
For a brief while
Yet you will be left
A pile of ashes
From the chambers of your heart
Burned to the ground by
The time the sun blinks at first awakening

The flowing of forgiveness and love
Quiets the flames in which we
So often of well-tread habit find solace
Dive into this river to be healed
It will take you to the ocean of the All
Merely a drop of blood
Running through the veins
Of God

Hanan –
Do not fear the Beautiful One
Her skin
Lips and
Breasts
Can you hug the moon's sweet white light
And yet be afraid of its caresses?
Can you kiss the sun's wakening warmth
Giver of life
Without open arms?

Hanan Says:

A heart that is closed and dead cannot be broken.
Heal my heart, Beloved
Then you may sunder it.

Hanan says:

God's voice
Follows the golden
Thread through your
Mind, oh Pilgrim
And if you
Allow it to echo
Out of your parched mouth
Without trying to hold it
That divine flow may quench all
Of our thirsts

Hanan says:

Hearing is relative.
Vibrations emit from her
Goddess mouth like a circus parade
Or a whirling dervish
Convention
Beckoning with their verdant cacophony of calls
And their honey-dipped tongues of lucid, sharp wisdom
From which my humble
Ears often only receive a tidbit
And for which my humble
Mouth may mutter
A "huh?"

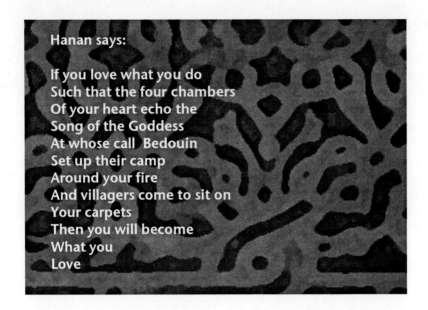

Hanan says:

If you love what you do
Such that the four chambers
Of your heart echo the
Song of the Goddess
At whose call Bedouin
Set up their camp
Around your fire
And villagers come to sit on
Your carpets
Then you will become
What you
Love

Hanan Says:

Can a man
Love two souls
At the same time?
As God forms and fills all of our hearts equally
The answer is yes.
However, given the proximity of said beings
This can make for
Very embarrassing
And unpleasant
Surprise visits.
Best to keep your knives and pans -
Oh expansive-hearted Pilgrim -
Under lock and key.

A pyramid of skulls
Is not a monument to
God
Yet the birds now nesting there
Still sing of
Figs and Flies
Dates and Dung
Weaving harmonies of life
As salve for
Those still wishing
To dance

Fireflies
Dance and float in festively adorned villages
As I hurl quietly
Less my bursts of laughter
Down the mountain path
Under the near-dark sky still dabbled with
Amorphous persimmon colored clouds
Stumbling
Through their flickering constellations
So
So happy to be alive...

Hanan thinks you would like this.

God winked once at
Hafez.
Hafez now spends the rest of his
Life
Winking back
By sticking his tongue out on paper.

Sometimes Hanan
Doesn't listen to God
And loses his way
Becoming very cranky,
Like whirlwinds on the desert plain
Wandering many directions from his path

Neither tea nor figs
Nor lamb nor qat nor opium
Give the appropriate directions home.

As the crow remembers its gathering place
Year upon year
So does the heart
Recall her bosom
And the hands that hold her always.

By seeing past our thoughts
We notice God's fingers already pointing
Where we needed to go.

Only one thing remains:
To grant yourself forgiveness
And start back on the way again.

Hanan says:

In the center of your heart
There is a house
And in this house
There is a room
And in this room
The mingling of song and chant
Prayer and silence,
Music and dance
Thought and being
Reflects the exchange of souls
Through which Consciousness
Forms itself, as it always knew it would

In the center of your heart
The seed of the All
The seed of the One
Grows into that which it already is and will be

Hanan Says:

Placing your finger in mouth's way
Of the animal used to food
Arriving into its field of vision
Is a quick recipe for
Tooth mark scars that your
Grandchildren will delight at querying you
About
Once they have followed your trail
Into this lifetime
To sit at your feet.

Weaving stories through your beard
Delight them with the untold ways
Of avoiding such permanent hand ornamentation
That is – unless –
They actually want it even more now.

Hanan says:

Sometimes mountains on the
Horizon
Melt away with the
Sunrise –
Even the camel
On which you sit
Was fooled by the clouds!

Interesting how
Something so ethereal
Can impersonate
That which is most solid

The Universal Mind
Plays tricks with
Mere humans
By likewise taking our forms
Leaving
It up to us
To remember and recognize
Our and each others'
Heavenliness
Even as we walk on the Earth

Hanan says:

There are some in this world
Who believe they are kings
Rather than pawns.

If they look at the tomb of Cyrus
And his fabled city of Persopolis
It may become clear
That the game of chess
For which they wager so much
Blood and gold
Is beyond their control.

As sure as the sun and moon
Chase each other far from our reach
It is God who built the board
On which they play
And she will put their
Pieces away and close
The drawer
As she sees fit.

Sometimes
Hanan sleeps with doubt
His heart-city's quarters
Besieged by armies
Looking for power, treasure and control
It is not until the golden emissaries
Of morning light
Dance past his lashes
Sneak under his lids and
Caress his eyes
That he awakens to the
Dream of life

In times of peril
Kin strife
And unsheathed scimitar
Many say, "It is not
Wise to speak one's mind,"
But what if the Heart
Controls the tongue?
And what if God controls
The Heart?

To those who would exterminate
A village like a
Lice-infested bazaar dog
Or with dark stealth
Through darker dealings
Enter the city gates to rob
Its peoples of life, know:

You cannot
Poke out
The eyes
Of God.

Do you know your roots
Fellow seeker?
Have you dug though the
Loam of this life
Into the bedrock of
Generations gone
Passing fossils and ancient bones along the way?

I have learned of "volcanoes"
From which the Earth's blood
Molten liquid stone
Surfaces...

Keep digging and you will find this fire
And singe your beard

Easier, is it not, to close your eyes
And ask your inner lineage directly
For the secret that is hardly one:
You are a child of God

Hanan is confused.
Again.
Stumbling drunk and blinded
By his own rough hands
Clasped in front of his eyes
Through today's maze of his own making.
Asking —
No, pleading — with God's bartender
To distill Life down to its clear essence
Of soul-expanding certitude
Having forgotten
It was freewheeling drink of said beverage
That got him in this perceived mess
To begin with.

What would Hanan say today?

To you Beloved,
After standing by the fire in the numbing air
Offering, then giving his honor and commitment
Even without certainty, and neither knowing nor
Claiming to fathom the
Depth
Width or
Height of the mysteries forming our conjoint
Dimensions,
The geometry of our feelings
The trajectory of our moments
The ultimate destination of our paths...

Hanan might just say this:
Let Us
Live Well,
Love Well,
Be Loved Well.

Hanan says:

Clutching the orchid
Only strips its petals
Grasping at angels
Only hurts their wings
Squeezing the pomegranate
Only creates a red puddle
Trying to control
The All
In your hands
Head
Even heart
Only likewise makes a mess

Please – God's cleaning lady has
Been on her feet since dawn –
Try to give her a rest!

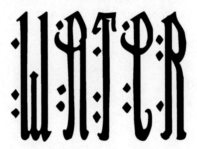

Hanan Says:

Feelings go away
Like ripples from a stone
Thrown in a pool of water
The larger we allow our pool to be
The more space it has to absorb
Our feelings

Trying to tighten that space
Holding on and controlling our feelings
Causes great waves of repercussion
Bouncing back and forth off our shores
Turbulence in our hearts
Delaying the return to placidness

It is the still pond
That best reflects the true essence
Of Heaven

Hanan Says:

Every moment with my Beloved
Is a pearl-dive into
The oft-clear yet uncharted dictionary of love
Learning new definitions
Of this simple and precious word
As noun
Verb
Adjective and
Adverb --
My vocabulary expands with leaps and bounds
In our joy and suffering,
Caresses and kisses.
My hands overflow with the treasure from these efforts --
Their palms face upwards
So you can better see and choose
Those jewels that make your heart sing.

A graceful heron
May stand at the river's edge
And look to the left.
There he sees and experiences that which is on the left
And then glances to the right
Where the choices open in that previous moment on the other
side
Are forever altered
Even as new ones now arrive on the right.
Yet his webbed feet remain unmoved
Solid in their touch of the mud below.

When we advance into the tide of opportunity
Swollen and seemingly treacherous
With currents of the Unknown
The great majority of our will and commitment
Is only needed to choose the moving towards
And to make that first step —
The Universe has already taken care of the rest
Such that our job
Is to be aware of the learning to be had and the feel
Of our feet on our path
Be it mud, stone or gold
Through that journey's moments
Each one a gift
In itself
Each one
Another piece of our selves.

Hanan Says:

Some people say that rain
Is the Divine's tears
Falling down from the Infinite
To cleanse us of our failings
In this human lifetime

I know nothing of God's tear ducts
Let alone her favorite colored handkerchief
But I wonder if the purveyors of this fine knowledge
Have ever lived in a desert?

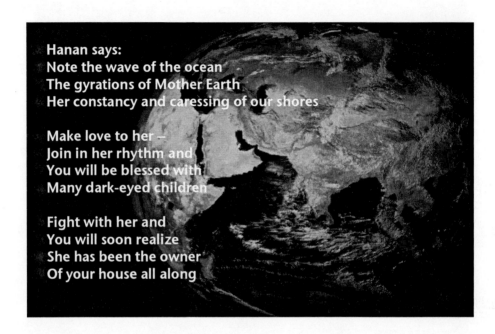

Hanan says:
Note the wave of the ocean
The gyrations of Mother Earth
Her constancy and caressing of our shores

Make love to her –
Join in her rhythm and
You will be blessed with
Many dark-eyed children

Fight with her and
You will soon realize
She has been the owner
Of your house all along

Words, words, words —
Alphabet-sired collections of
What I can say
What you can write down
Barely
Hold the hunger for the Beloved
Momentarily in their well-intended grasping.

Blink and the wave of feeling is already out to sea,
Bound for wherever the horizon finally decides to settle.

There are those moments
Swimming in his deep and turbulent ocean of hubris
When Hanan
In spite of knowing that he is ultimately talking about himself
Wants to say this
To the all-knowing
All-connecting source of
Love and existence:
"Please stop fucking with me!"

Hanan says:

To make a divine tea
Do the following:
In a large vessel
Add hot water
Sea salt
And herbs of your choosing.
Steep yourself in consciousness,
Allowing steam wisps to
Dance off the surface and
Return to
The mother clouds
Serving as God's
Eyelids above
Blinking shadows
And bring into relief
The diverse terrain of humanity.

60

Love has been there
Since the beginning of time -
Love in fact
Is the reason
For this
Existence
For this
Creation
That was conceived
And birthed
Ages ago
And every moment since

Even in the
Rupturing of my heart
Even in the
Drowning of my soul
In tears
I recall
Being with my Beloved
Being one with Love
Feeling utterly whole
Then stopping
A moment
To breathe
To honor this temporal suffering
No less real, no less painful for its passing
This apparent separation
This "this"
That itself is only an exhale of God
And if I pay closer attention
I would see through our human veil
The Beloved winking at me
Through my own eyes
Reminding me of the joy we will share together
Having shed this incarnation
At our return to the All.

Beloved,
You are more the rose hip than
The rose
I make a tea of you
Drinking you in
With all senses awake
Infused with your
Liquid soul

Seeking:

Among cypress shadows
The teapot whistles
On the campfire
Your blood is boiling
With God circulating
Through your veins
Your left little toe shakes in the ecstasy
Of searching and being found
With every beat of your heart

Hanan says:

As each year has its seasons
So the Heart
From day to day
Moment to moment
Will know winters

Ice forms on the sides of
Rivers in the shallows
Where currents slow and
Reeds, branches and debris call home

Such is it with our Souls —
When our paths keep us
Deep enough in our being
Swimming in the strong flow of God
We do not
Become caught in
Inevitable obstructions
Of the mundane edges
Considered to be existence

Where do the fish play in winter?
They dance and cavort
Sending up angel-bubbles
In the deepest spots
Of river, lake and pond

Hanan Says:

The bursting swollen peach
Of the Universe
Yelled at me last night:
"Stop playing with poems and
Fuck me you fool!"

Hanan says:
I cannot sleep
When God is raining down
Torrents of awareness
Through the feeble tent-flaps
Of my mind
Reft open again
No matter how tight I tied them

I will not rest
Until hours of headstands later
My mind has mopped up the
Constellations and reflected universe
Of every puddle

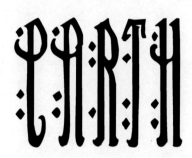

Hanan says:

Your warm breath
On my ear
In the morning
Is like the dew of the Goddess
Waking the Earth
For a new day

Hanan says:

The sand dune
Whirls tambur tunes with wind and sky
Appearing as one thing
Even as it is a
Composite of uncountable grains
Each of which may
Over many of our lifetimes
Come from different distant mountains
Just think:
A grain at the bottom of the dune
Defines it
As much as a grain on its ridge
Though crows, caravans and camels
Yea, the sun's own visage
Will never see that grain
Dormant in the dune's depths
Yet it is that piece of sand
That allows the dune
To stand as tall as it does

Hanan says:

Let us find a Zoroastrian
Up on the Peak of Zard Kuh mountain
Measuring the pin-holes of the night sky's curtain
And the devout servant of Mohammed
Bowing prostrate ever west
In Nasir al-Molk mosque
And the Buddhist monk
Cross-legged in silent meditation
Under the Bhodi tree

Fellow seeker,
Which one knows the way to find God?

None is better than the other.
The All sets its roots and
Uncurls its tendrils of awareness
In every soil
So long as the heart-gardener
Knows the crop
Is already
Ripe for the harvest

Hanan Says:

Your cold hands
Gently ask for warmth
Under God's night eye
Watching us
Explore our temporal
And unified terrain
The landscape of which
Stretches taut over our souls
Reducing to a sliver of moonlight
The difference between us

Hanan says:

Enough with your
Search for perfection –
Your wandering the desert of details and analysis
With parched heart and drowning mind.
Enough already!
Sit down under this date palm and drink
In the shade and comfort of knowing that
God crafted you and
That which you create
Long before
And long after
The heat of today's sun
And that she is, was
And will be
Pleased with the results
She winks at you,
Perfection-seeker,
Only to grab your attention
And lead you to the oasis
You never actually left.

Hanan says:

Give birth to yourself
Every day
Let the cosmos be your midwife
As you squeeze through
The vagina of experience.

Oh seeker, allow yourself
To leave Ego's womb —
Poke your head out...
Drink in the sunshine
Do not fear the light

Playing the Damam
Pulse of the encampment
The Setar with its three strings
Sings vibration choruses
That on a good night
Seduce the Beloved
Under your blankets
And otherwise
Rouse the dogs
To moonless night
Harmonizing

Hanan says:

The simple man spends
His time under the sky
The purple-blue
Tent
Night's curtain
And awakens to
The fire
Of God's eye

Eyelids succumb to gravity's call
Then not
Allowing for the creation of
Half-seen poetry
Flowing from day-weary fingers
Sustained only by
Feelings of you, Beloved
Emanating from the chambers of my heart
Rippling out, into and through
My soul, my body, my mind.
My how you
Have become that which
Was and is worth longing for
All along
Deepening your roots
In the fertile soil that is our love
Picturing our home -
Close your eyes and see it now:
Its hearth warmed by fire
In the cool evening of early spring
As the pinhole-stars of heaven's blanket
Appear above
Children of various sizes play nearby
Filling the space with laughter and
More joy than even our mutual adoration
Could ever have wished
I rub your back
And bedtime passes
Leaving us alone and together
To breathe in each others'
Words and touches

Silence and desires
Loving well
Fiercely and gently both
Enthralled and invested in every moment
Until there are no more
Until we rejoin our source.
God smiles,
Pleased with that day's journey
And return.

Hanan Says:

On the day your shadow became heavy
You tried leaving your path behind
God sat back to watch you
Knowing you were not as lost
As your thought-besieged mind
Echoed
Tempting you with glory to be had
As if God's wine was not enough
As if her tea was poison

Listen:
Listen to the unchanged story
Of your life
The whispers and wisps
Are there always
Only asking for a little moment of quiet
So they may sneak in
Through the backdoor to your heart

Pilgrim:

Why bar the portico to your soul?

In this world there exist
So many stories and songs
More sides than a sphere
Slippery in olive oil
Unable to be grasped
By your locked fists

Open your hands
Plant your sandaled feet
And ponder
Whose music should you dance to?

The Beloved is already humming
Her part
Of your age-old duet

Hanan says:

What is it to bow so exactingly
On your carpets towards Mecca
At the minarets' call
When between reverent recitations
You pilfer oranges from the market
Slander neighbors over grazing
Blind or make mute brothers
To keep them from your gilded chair?
Oh devout one, remember:
The house of the All
Is the house of all
And we are simply tenants

Hanan says:

Look at the artisans
Translators of beauty
Who
In these lower realms
Are vessels
Containing the many forms and faces of the All
Spilling out their contents
With ink and song
Chisel and paint

As tea is poured into cup
Its essence drawn from
Leaves
Plant
Birth-seed and
Soil in which it had rested
So God flows through our teapots

Drink without fear
Let a chorus of gratefulness and gusto
Echo about your heart's hallways and chambers

Hanan Says:

Breathe in your troubles
Weary traveler
Take them deep into your lungs
So they may absorb into your
Being
Exhale echoing
Sighs and see the signs —

God's own wish
Asks you to accept stillness
That your donkey mind
Settles and stops
Kicking up so much dust
Clouding the air about the garden
Hiding its cultivated beauty

Eggplant and peas taste far less interesting
All coated in dirt

Hanan Says:

Be clear about
Your obscurations
Be near with
Your separations
And know
Dear seeker
That as you
Hold out your cup
God is both the alms
You receive
And the giver thereof

Hanan Says:

Longing forlorn for the Beloved
Crying on your knees
In the moment you cannot take any more pain
A whisper comes to your ear from a passing butterfly
Reminding you:

Be with the longing -
Allow it to bloom
And bear fruit
The seed of which is the seed of God
In you

Hanan Says:

Exhale, heart, exhale.
Feel the desire, feel.
Do not for even a second
Allow mischievous Mind and
Its 10 distant accomplices
To set themselves to the task
Of building kingdoms of thought and words
However grand they may seem and appear
To foreign visitors, local audiences and vassals of your domain.
Listen:
Hot and sweaty children are frivolously playing in the alley
Emitting exuberant words unknown in any written language
Except in the parlance of raw Joy
And Love
And Life...
Put down your pen
Go roll around in the dirt with your emotional playmates -
And please don't waste your time by calling them names!

Hanan Says:

We are all the same.
How do I know this?
When I trace my lines
Back beyond my parents and their parents
Into time's fading memory
The source of Me in this moment
Becomes diffuse as it widens out as does the hourglass
Yet the more people it includes
The greater the number of those who
Are connected to you and him and her
By way of sisters and brothers and cousins
Aunts, Uncles and Great-Great somebodies
All sitting on the floor commenting on
The qualities of my cooking
And choice of tea.

Hanan is feeling cozier already!

Hanan Says:

Longing –
Attachment to Love
Is the beautiful and sharp
Double-edged
Damascene-hammered sword
Held in God's hands
Cutting through the milieu
The confusion
The ongoing battle that
Is this life's incarnation
Releasing
In sometimes almost-lethal spurts
The blood of
Love, joy and pain
Suffering and ecstasy
While we stand together by the fire,
After our caravans have separated,
And every moment in between.

I could name and rename constellations after you each night
So that my memory's thirsty cup would be ever refreshed
By glancing upwards
Yet barely feel quenched.

Being in the presence and radiance of
Your smile, Beloved,
Is utterly worth the scars and scabs
Nicks and notches

That come with
Having thrown away our shields and sheaths
Throwing open our hearts instead

Hanan Says:

What is the difference between
Jumping and falling?
Usually we choose to jump
Or so we think —
And often we arrive at the same
Location, either way.

Hanan Says:

Clouds
Birthing and rebirthing themselves
In Sky's womb
Frame the view from here
Even as hope for their blessing
Seems as barren
As the surroundings
Where we have stopped to rest.
I sit – tail wagging in canine admiration and joy
At the possibility of
What may come
Whether now or soon
So aptly defined by God
Regardless of my
Attempts at measuring it
In shadow's arcs or grains fallen
Thankful for the Grace in this moment
And the moment itself.

Yearning for beginners:

As the breeze momentarily caresses the leaf
Never to touch it again
As the raindrop passes through that wisp of wind
Before it joins the earth
As the ground feels my Beloved's supple feet
Alter it with slight pressure
On the way back to her house
Perhaps not to be with me
As I leave on my journey
For minutes, moons or millennia...
Does it really matter?
For she has already
Caressed my heart
Joined with my soul
And altered my self
Such that no time or travel
Removes her from me
Or cleanses the longing for her
That dances and spins
In every grain of my being

Hanan Says:

The vagabond poet's currency is words
Words and the breath that carries them...
I have learned that in the Spanish realm
Once part of the Moorish empire Al-Andalus
They have new words in their language
One of many children from this perhaps unwilling
Yet seven hundred yearlong matrimony
That, we can all agree, is ending quite badly.
The power of words has indeed caused wars and destruction
Beyond reason
Among nations
Brothers
Friends
Lovers
Yet sometimes we mortals create beauty, like the bastard
offspring *Ojalá*
Which, in Spain is taken to mean "Let's hope"
And in our tongue, though with an additional letter or two, "As
God wills"
Bringing two hostile cultures' ire into symmetry
As God *is* Hope *is* God
Now I do not claim to know which lineage should clothe
And feed and find work for
Such a child
But let us hope he lives a full and useful life, as God would will it.

Hanan doesn't know what to say
About losing this love.
Hanan beats his chest
From the outside even as his chest pounds him within
As he wails to God:
Why? Why? Why?
Why did you give me this path
Of chasm-deep joy, desire and connection
With such a beautiful Friend
Allowing my heart to alight, walking on stars
To dance and sing
Drunk with You
Yet seeing the rest of this lifetime so clearly
Only to envelop my way in a sandstorm of change
Darkening the sky as if filled with thousands of arrows
My heart the lonely target
Turning the solidness of this Love
Into mirage?
As the storm settles you leave Hanan
Standing alone in the barrens
Making him find, no be,
His own oasis
And in that dear spot
Remember that you, sweet Friend
Were the Beloved incarnated
To walk with me on this journey
For a million moments
To teach me how real
Love can be
To accept the precious nature of life
And re-learn the invaluableness of my very self.

Hanan Says:

Sleep now, Pilgrim.
The soles of your mind
Have treaded far today
Encountered many obstacles
And taken on a few well-placed blisters...
It is time now to rest —
Even the birds have put their choruses to bed.
Return to bathe in the flow of Grace
For which there is no price and
In which you must do nothing — only be.

Hanan Says:

The twin
Serpent-heads
Of Love and Lust
Fight over you,
Beloved -
Sometimes together,
Sometimes against
Each other
Encircling you worshipfully yet voraciously
Offering themselves completely
At your supple feet
Even as they seek to
Join and devour you.

Humble I do not so much wish to
Choose
Yet if choice is required
How does one tell these poised Cobras
Rattle-ready to strike
And inflict their potent venom
Of feeling and desire
Upon my undefended Heart
That I only will receive one set of fangs?

Truth is:
I was bitten the day I was born a man.
Only now midway through this summer
Has the antidote presented itself
In the incarnation of you.

Know:

We are the Beloved -
The Beloved is Hanan
The Beloved is You
The Beloved is Always

As the dawn-light
Eases its way into the clouded sky
After a night of storms
I feel tired, yet alive

How else could one feel
After being tossed about
In the rough-and-tumble playground
Of the mind
By a visiting band of God's voices
Like so many tornadoes
Spawned of the pregnant clouds
Making momentary and devastating links
Between Heaven and Earth

The head and its contents ache –
Kicked out instead of kicked in by
Divine feet
On a mission to make room
For a bee's wing weight
Honeycomb sweet
Of the All

Sometimes Hanan
Just wants to say that something is "beautiful":
A cloud, a person, a feeling
A conversation with God –
Without having to be a slave to
Allegory, hyperbole or analogy
Without wording it all in sweeping statements
Of mystic philosophy, religion or personal psychosis.
Sometimes Hanan allows himself that distinct pleasure.

You,
Dear Friend,
Are beautiful.

HISTORY & CONTEXT

Hanan al Hannan (ca. 1295-1375) was a little known contemporary of Shams al-Din Hafez (ca. 1320-1390), the great Persian mystical poet from Shiraz. Like Hafez, Hanan al Hannan was at least on the surface a Shiite Moslem strongly influenced by Sufism and its elaborate system of symbolism and pantheism.

In the Sufi belief system, each human soul is a particle of the Divine Absolute, and the mystic aims at a complete union with this Divine. This union is attained in the knowledge that a human being is himself that ultimate reality which he seeks. Only by seeing things as they truly are and abandoning the structural restraints of conventional culture and religion can he or she attain this higher goal.

Little is known about Hanan's early life. It has been said that Hanan came east from the remnants of Crusader states in erstwhile Palestine with his Islamic mother after the death of his father, who likely had Nestorian Christian beliefs. Along the way, his mother also died or abandoned the journey and one account describes that Hanan "appeared with the wind from the West" in southern Persia circa 1338, along a trade route that connected the Arab Empire with Damascus and the sea beyond. It is noted that he survived the months-long trek using little more than an

100

uncommon speech, which drew meaning and connected words to deliver poetry and prose such that it would beguile those within hearing to aid the impoverished wanderer. Some thought him an unstable magician with roots in and exposure to Islam, Zoroastrian traditions and fringe Christianity, using words to weave spells, trances and illusions. If anything, Hanan, as described by those of his era who claimed to have spent time with him, was viewed as an eclectic and often humorous presenter of ideas some of which bordered on treasonous depending on the audience.

It is said that Hanan al Hannan first met Hafez in the terrace of the *Jame'e Atig* Mosque, equally inspired by the deep spiritual roots of the location and past use as a Zoroastrian ceremonial site. Historians have not verified this meeting, but merchant accounts from the late 1350's report a gathering in the open land between Esfahan and Yazd at which both Hanan and Hafez were present and engaged in a "divine exchange of God's breath" while dancing in a trance state from dusk until dawn. There are no records of what was said that night, and there are no other accounts of interaction between the two men.

Where Hafez remained stationary for most of his life, Hanan served as an itinerant bard and seer, wandering mostly among the smaller villages of the Fars region and appending himself to caravans reported to have brought him as far as India to the East where he came into direct contact with Buddhist teachings, further influencing his poetry and disposition. He practiced swordsmanship, often trading verbal blows among parleys and jabs in caravan camps. The crusades of the previous century and expanding Tamerlane (*Timur-i lang*) and Ottoman Empires preoccupied Hanan, and he spoke of war in spontaneous lectures, trying to sway those who listened to not pick up the scimitar and engage in killing over "what God is or is not", making him a target to emerging powers and reinforcing his persistent movement and relatively obscure status. Eventually he traveled back West to Palestine or Lebanon to further spread a message of tolerance where he passed into the next realm under unknown circumstances.

Due to his outspoken and anti-establishment nature, works by Hanan may have been cited to mystics or poets of other names at various times – indeed, Hanan may have used a dozen or more "names" throughout his lifetime to ensure his survival. The included works, as revealed, primarily reflect the pre-Tamerlane period of his poetry, most of which begins with the phrase "Hanan says:" serving as his oral signature. His spoken words and poetry fall within the lyrical and mystical traditions of his era and are meant to be understood (or perhaps *mis*understood) on various levels, depending on the individual reader and their connection to "the All".

While they wrote and orated poetry in the same region of the world over concurrent decades, a comparison between Hafez and Hanan indicates a relationship somewhat akin to that of Emerson and Thoreau. Simply put, Hanan, like Thoreau, was more immersed in the praxis of living and experiencing – he viewed his time on Earth as perhaps many see Hafez' love-driven 40 day meditation on the mountaintop. While Hanan wandered as a way of life as meteor showers appear and retreat, Hafez was more sedentary, fixed and dependable like the sun. Accordingly, the insights of Hanan may appear to the reader as chaotic, but do not be mistaken. Like his justly esteemed and revered poetic peer, Hanan's works are essentially single-minded of focus: God (the All, the One, the Universe) is in and is each of us, period. Everything Hanan interpreted through his senses, perceptions and historical and cultural context of his time is parlayed through words derived from his sense that we are all connected, seed, root, stem and flower to each other and that we are not as separate as we perceive.

The rapidly changing base of knowledge and experience in southern Persia as a crossroads of commerce, politics, culture, language, religion, spirituality and local, regional and (at that time) global conflict and power struggle serve to inform Hanan's poetry as well as define its relevance today. The Middle East and world in general appear to be in a state of flux and conflict in the 21st Century bearing great and grave similarities to Hanan's time. Escalating warfare and attempted conquests among nations and sub-groups using a self-determined proprietary definition of God to create differences and distance from the "other" in order to justify their actions echo the Crusades – the likely reason for Hanan's forced abandonment of the Palestine region and the start of his quest for understanding.

The suffering under Tamerlane, who co-opted Islam to better serve his imperial greed and expansion goals, reminds one immediately of rulers on either side of current conflicts who use belief systems to achieve their means without, unfortunately, practicing the tenets at the spiritual heart of those philosophies. Many are those sent to war under false pretenses who go because they are told, but understand little that the opposing side is so very much like them in just another misperceived form. Hanan is preoccupied with these elements of human experience and clearly feels the loss to the All of such activity. Hanan's wishes, as expressed in his poetry, are that we all in some way (and he does not claim to know the specific path) seek to fulfill the potentiality of human existence.

Hanan's work clearly forsakes traditional Ghazals and explores what is referred to today as "colloquial poetry". Of the traditional foci, meter, and rhythms of Persian poetry, Hanan only worked with variations on two forms: The *purposeful poem* (Ghassideh), and *fragments* (Ghattehaat). The translations as revealed remain as true as possible to his unadorned way of delivering the insights and perceptions as he interpreted them with and within the Universe.

Using his quirky perspectives and off-beat simple jests, Hanan is saying that in finding our own paths to ourselves, we better come to know the paths of the others with whom we share time and space. Inevitably, we see that we are all strands of the Universe, woven together by the All for reasons we may never fully comprehend.